The Joy of Being a Eucharistic Minister

The Joy of Being a Eucharistic Minister

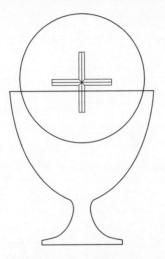

Mitch Finley

Resurrection Press
Mineola • New York

Nihil Obstat:
REV. MARK F. PAUTLER, JCL
Censor Librorum
December 18, 1997
Spokane, Washington

Imprimatur
✠ MOST REVEREND WILLIAM S. SKYLSTAD
Bishop of Spokane
December 22, 1997
Spokane, Washington

First published in March, 1998 by Resurrection Press, Ltd.
　　　　　　　　　　　　P.O. Box 248, Williston Park, NY 11596

ISBN 1-878718-45-2　　Library of Congress Catalog Card Number 97-75614

All Bible quotations are from the New Revised Standard Version Bible: Catholic Edition, Copyright 1989, 1993, Division of Christian Education of the National Council of the Churches of Christ in the United States of America.

Excerpts from the English translation of *The Catechism of the Catholic Church* for use in the United States of America Copyright © 1994 United States Catholic Conference, Inc.— Libreria Editrice Vaticana. Used with Permission.

Cover design by John Murello. Printed in the United States of America.

Acknowledgments

The author extends sincere thanks
to the many eucharistic ministers
he has known over the years,
whose example has been an inspiration
for this book.

CONTENTS

Introduction

You Are "Extraordinary"!

CONGRATULATIONS! Since you are reading this small book that means you are—or are thinking about becoming—a eucharistic minister. To be more precise, in the official language of the church you are—or are thinking about becoming—an "extraordinary minister of the eucharist."

In 1973, diocesan bishops were authorized to commission Catholic laity to distribute Communion during Mass and take Communion to the sick or dying. Sometimes eucharistic ministers are also commissioned to preside at Communion services in the absence of a priest. The appointment to be an extraordinary minister of the eucharist may be either permanent or limited to a specific period of time.

The HarperCollins Encyclopedia of Catholicism explains: "The principle supporting this 'extraordinary ministry' is outlined in the 1983 Code of Canon Law (can. 230.3), which states that laypeople can exercise the ministry of the word, preside over liturgical prayers, confer Baptism and distribute Holy Communion whenever the needs of the Church require it, or whenever sufficient ordained ministers are not available."

As official church documents use the term, "extraordinary" means "out of the ordinary," the ordinary in this case being a priest or deacon. As a layperson, it is "out of the ordinary" for you to give Communion to others, so that makes you an "extraordinary" minister of the eucharist. There is another meaning to the word "extraordinary," however, and you should apply that meaning to yourself, as well.

According to a dictionary, "extraordinary" can also mean "highly exceptional or remarkable." This meaning fits you perfectly. As a volunteer ready to distribute Holy Communion during parish Masses you present yourself in service to the faith community. That makes you a highly exceptional person. As a volunteer who is prepared to carry Holy Communion to those who are sick, dying, or confined to their homes for whatever reason, you are a remarkable person, indeed.

As an extraordinary minister of the eucharist —from now on we'll use the shorthand term, "eucharistic minister"—you serve the faith community in a way that is both a great privilege and a form of humble service. You distribute to others the consecrated bread and/or wine which has become the "body and blood, soul and divinity" of the risen Christ. You become one who serves, a servant, someone whose purpose is to nourish those who turn to the risen Lord for the nourishment only he can give.

The spirituality of the eucharistic minister is bound to be shaped by this special ministry, and that brings up the main purpose for this book. The ritual which launches eucharistic ministers in their special ministry is called the "Order for the Commissioning of Extraordinary Ministers of Holy Communion." There are two options for this ritual, the "Order of Commissioning Within Mass," and the "Order of Commissioning Within a Celebration of the Word of God." In the latter option, the priest or deacon addresses those chosen to be eucharistic ministers, and among his remarks are the following words:

> In this ministry, you must be examples of Christian living in faith and conduct; you must strive to grow in holiness through this sacrament of unity and love. Remember that, though many, we are one body because we share the one bread and one cup.
>
> As ministers of holy communion be, therefore, especially observant of the Lord's

command to love your neighbor. For when he gave his body as food to his disciples, he said to them: "This is my commandment, that you should love one another as I have loved you."

The purpose of this book is to offer some tips and insights on a spirituality for eucharistic ministers, at the heart of which is love for God and neighbor. This is not a practical guide on "how to" be a eucharistic minister. Rather, this book is meant to nourish the heart and soul of anyone who is a eucharistic minister and encourage deeper intimacy with the risen Christ present in the eucharist.

Ideally, when you finish reading this book you will have a better understanding of what it means to be a eucharistic minister, and you will feel a deeper joy in being a eucharistic minister yourself.

Those who eat my flesh
and drink my blood
have eternal life,
and I will raise them up
on the last day;
for my flesh is true food
and my blood is true drink.
Those who eat my flesh
and drink my blood
abide in me, and I in them.
Just as the living Father sent me,
and I live because of the Father,
so whoever eats me
will live because of me.

JOHN 6:54-57

Chapter 1

The Eucharist Is a Joyful Mystery

IN APRIL OF 1994, *The New York Times* and *CBS News* polled a representative sampling of Catholics in the United States. Of those surveyed, 34 percent said they believe the bread and wine consecrated at Mass "become the body and blood of Christ." Sixty-three percent, however, said they believe that the consecrated bread and wine are merely "symbolic reminders of Jesus." Only among Catholics 65 and older did a small majority—51 to 45 percent—say that at Mass the bread and wine are "changed into Christ's body and blood."

In 1997, a similar survey of parishes in the Diocese of Rochester, New York, had similar results. Sixty to 65 percent of the Catholics polled said that they do not believe the bread and wine "become the body and blood of Christ." These results were consistent from parish to parish and among all age groups.

There seems to be considerable misunderstanding of the eucharist among Catholics in our time. To say that the eucharistic bread and wine become the body and blood of Christ is not a mere analogy or metaphor. The *Catechism of the Catholic Church* could not be more clear: "At the heart of the eucharistic celebration are the bread and wine that, by the word of Christ and the invocation of the Holy Spirit, become Christ's Body and Blood. . . . The signs of bread and wine become, in a way surpassing understanding, the Body and Blood of Christ. . ." (No. 1333).

This is the ancient faith of the church, the faith of the followers of Christ since the earliest days of the Christian community. In his First Letter to the Corinthians, which scholars date to about A.D. 54, St. Paul reminds his readers: "The cup of blessing that we bless, is it not a sharing in the blood of Christ? The bread that we break, is it not a sharing in the body of Christ?" (10:16).

We should not be too hard on Catholics who do not believe that the eucharistic bread and wine become the actual "body and blood, soul and divinity" of Christ. Perhaps not only they, but all of us, are not as well informed about the eucharist as we could be. Perhaps Catholics who do not accept the conventional description of the eucharist simply want to be honest, and the conventional formula no longer "works" for them.

Perhaps those of us who do accept the conventional formula about the bread and wine becoming the "body and blood" of Christ sometimes wonder what this actually *means*. As eucharistic ministers, it is especially important for us to seek as complete and accurate an understanding of the eucharist as we can.

It is possible that by simply repeating the phrase "body and blood" over and over, insisting that this is what the bread and wine become, we have lost touch with the deeper truth of the eucharist. Like all religious language, "body and blood of Christ" is an attempt to put into human words a mystery the human intellect can never fully grasp. Perhaps it will be helpful if we take two steps back, look at what we are talking about, and see if we can spark some new life in the old words. Gradually, we may find ourselves faced with a Great Mystery, and appropriately so.

It is important to understand that *"body and blood" is a Semitic phrase that means "the whole person."* When we say that the bread and wine of the Mass become the "body and blood" of Christ, we say that the bread and wine become the "whole person" of Christ. Catholicism insists that following the consecration the whole person of Christ is present in both the bread and the wine. Only a sacramental simple-mindedness will view the bread as Christ's body, the wine as his blood, and never the twain shall meet.

This is why for many generations Catholics received Communion only in the form of bread while the priest alone drank from the chalice. This is why, even today, in certain instances a person may receive Communion only from the cup—someone whose illness prevents him or her from swallowing a consecrated host, for example. Also, it is still not unusual for many Catholics to receive only the host at Communion, even when the consecrated wine is available. In both cases, though receiving only the bread, or only the wine, the person really and truly receives the "whole person" of Christ—"body and blood, soul and divinity"—in Communion.

Perhaps those who say they do not believe that the bread and wine become the "body and blood" of Christ are trying to say that they no longer find meaning in the phrase "body and blood." Perhaps they think they have no choice but to take this phrase literally, in a physical sense that borders on the gruesome. Our era has been so heavily shaped by the human sciences, including psychology, that perhaps the phrase "whole person" will make more sense, and be more acceptable, to more people. If we explain that "body and blood" means "whole person," perhaps that will help clarify the meaning of the eucharistic presence of Christ.

We need to remind ourselves, as well, that in the eucharist we do not receive the historical, flesh-and-blood Jesus. Continually repeating the "body and blood" phrase, without explanation, may not only mislead some people, it may also reinforce the misconception that the Christ we receive in Communion, in the consecrated bread and wine, is Jesus as he walked the dusty roads of Palestine, or Jesus as he hung on the cross. This simply is not true.

The Christ we receive in the eucharist is, indeed, the one who lived, taught, and died in first-century Palestine. But the Christ we receive in the consecrated bread and wine is much more than that. The Christ we receive is the *risen* Christ who is with us now, alive and active in the Church and in the world. It is the "body and blood, soul and divinity," the "whole person" of the *risen* Christ that we receive in Holy Communion.

With this realization we find ourselves smack in the middle of an overwhelmingly profound mystery, an experience of transcendent holiness, a sacred event of awesome dimensions. When we receive Communion, and when we as eucharistic ministers give Communion to others, if we have even an inkling of what we are about, we may be inclined to fall on our faces in wonder and worship.

In the eucharist, and in Holy Communion, we find ourselves at the heart of the mystery upon which Christian faith is ultimately founded —the Resurrection of the Lord Jesus. "If there is no resurrection of the dead, then Christ has not been raised," St. Paul says; "and if Christ has not been raised, then our proclamation has been in vain and your faith has been in vain" (1 Cor 15:13-14).

In *The Resurrection of Jesus* (Paulist Press, 1997), theologian Father Kenan B. Osborne, O.F.M., emphasizes that the Resurrection of Jesus is ultimately an incomprehensible mystery:

> Whoever claims to understand [the Resurrection] or name it cannot be said to have really understood or named the un-ending mystery. The Christian belief in the resurrection is just such a mystery: it. . . can never be understood fully nor named clear-ly. Church leaders, whether ecclesiastical or theological, can only point to the mystery and describe it in an insufficient way.

If we say, therefore, as we must, that in the eucharist we receive the whole person of the *risen*

Christ, we find ourselves face-to-face with a supernatural mystery of overwhelming transcendence and sacredness. How can we not tremble—figuratively if not literally—at the thought of what the risen Lord does for us in giving us himself in Holy Communion? How can we not see our role as eucharistic ministers as a privilege to be wondered at?

There is no room for a casual attitude toward the eucharist, even in the most informal Mass. There is only room for gratitude, respect, and thanksgiving. Earlier generations had a deep respect for the presence of the eucharistic Christ on the altars and in the tabernacles of their parish churches, a sense of gratitude and worship that later generations sometimes seem to misplace. The more we reflect on the mystery of the Resurrection and its intimate relationship with the Blessed Sacrament, however, the more likely we are to regain an appropriate spirit of eucharistic awe and worship.

Yet there is still more we must reflect upon with regard to the mystery of the Resurrection. What can we say about the risen Christ whom we receive in Holy Communion? We receive the "body and blood" or "whole person" of the risen Christ in Communion. But what is a "risen" person, and what can his "body and blood" be in its "risen" condition? What is it we receive but the gift and promise of eternal life? The mystery only increases. . .

Father Osborne offers another helpful observation:

> The resurrection of Jesus must be seen not simply as life after death. More fundamentally, it is life in God, life with God, life in God's love and peace, after death. It is this "in God" and this "with God" which characterizes the risen life far more than the "after death" aspect. Jairus's daughter, the son of the widow at Nain, and Lazarus all had life "after death." What they did not have was "risen" life, or a distinctive way of human living "with God" and "in God." By saying this I wish to argue that the human nature of Jesus, which through the hypostatic union was already "united" to God, came to be in a special way even more intimately "united" to God: (a) through moments of prayer, during his earthly life, and (b) through the special event called resurrection.

Father Osborne adds: "God's activity in the resurrection event was not merely a raising of Jesus from the dead; it was far more profoundly a raising of Jesus' humanity into an intimacy with

God's own life which Jesus' humanity, up to that time, had never experienced before."

When we receive Holy Communion, then, when we receive the "whole person" of the risen Christ, what we consume is the "whole person" of the Son of God who carried his humanity, and ours, into the most complete intimacy with God possible through his own Resurrection.

We receive nourishment from the "whole person"—"body and blood, soul and divinity"—of the risen Christ who, because of his Resurrection, has a human and divine union with God beyond anything we can begin to imagine. This is the risen Christ who gives himself to us in the eucharist. This is the risen Christ we, as eucharistic ministers, give to others. If reflection on this profound mystery does not lead to speechless prayer, nothing will.

In the eucharist we receive the whole person of the risen Christ. But recall what Jesus says in the Gospel of John, in the account of the raising of Lazarus from death: "I am the resurrection. . ." (11:25).

The risen Jesus is himself the Resurrection, therefore in Holy Communion we receive the power of Jesus' Resurrection so that his Resurrection and our own future resurrection have an impact on us and on our life today. The divine mystery of the Resurrection, this grace, this special life "in God" and "for God" nourishes us here and now in the eucharist. Even now we experience the future in the form of our own resurrection in Christ!

One of the great things about the eucharist, however, is that no matter what we say we find ourselves immediately obliged to say more. One truth leads to another and another. As Catholics we believe that in Communion we receive as nourishment for our whole self the whole person of the risen Christ. The traditional term for this is the "real presence." But Catholics believe that Christ is really present in other ways, as well.

The Second Vatican Council, in the mid-1960s, declared that Christ is present "not only" in the person of the priest who presides in Christ's name, "but especially in the eucharistic species," that is, in the consecrated bread and wine. Christ is also present "in his word since it is he himself who speaks when the holy Scriptures are read in the Church." Christ is present "when the Church prays and sings, for he has promised 'where two or three are gathered together in my name there am I in the midst of them (Mt. 18:20).' " (*Constitution on the Sacred Liturgy*, no. 7.)

"Now you," St. Paul says, "are the body of Christ and individually members of it" (1 Cor

12:27). Through Baptism we are incorporated into the body of Christ, a community that exists in this world and the next, in both time and eternity. Because we are the body of Christ, Christ is present in the assembly or congregation when we gather for Mass. Indeed, it is because the risen Christ is present in our midst, in the community of faith, that he becomes really present in the eucharist. At the same time, he becomes present in our midst, in a unique way, because he is present in the consecrated bread and wine.

This is why the eucharist is not a spectator activity. Everyone participates in the ritual, the whole community celebrates the eucharist; in a very real sense the entire congregation "says Mass." The priest presides, to be sure, and only he has the authority and power to consecrate the bread and wine so they become the "whole person" of the risen Christ. But theologically the priest cannot celebrate the eucharist apart from the community of faith where Christ is present. Even in the rare instance where a priest may say Mass with no one else present, he does so only through his spiritual union with the whole Church.

What is the relevance of this insight to the activities of a eucharistic minister? In the context of the Mass itself the eucharistic minister's role is obvious. He or she helps to distribute Communion, and the communal or congregational context is evident to everyone. Eucharistic ministers who take Communion to shut-ins or those who are sick may seem, however, to be individuals involved in an individualistic ministry. On the contrary, such eucharistic ministers are representatives of the entire parish community and should think of themselves as such.

A eucharistic minister who brings Communion to sick or shut-in members of the parish brings the "whole person" or "body and blood" of the risen Christ, the same Christ who dwells in the midst of and constitutes the heart of the parish community. Therefore, when we bring Communion to those unable to come to their parish church for Mass, we bring them the risen Christ who is present in a special way in the consecrated host but in the community of faith, as well. We also bring Christ present in his word when we read the scriptural passages that are a part of the Communion ritual.

When we visit someone who is shut-in or confined to a hospital, therefore, it is particularly important for eucharistic ministers to think of themselves not as a mere delivery service for Holy Communion. Rather, as a eucharistic minister you bring in your own person the parish community and the risen Christ who is present there. In a very real sense, as a eucharistic minister you yourself become a kind of "sacrament," a carrier of God's loving presence for the person to whom you bring Communion.

The early 20th-century French Catholic poet, Leon Bloy, once said: "Joy is the most infallible sign of the presence of God." Some people seem to think that the most infallible sign of the presence of God is a kind of grim solemnity. For such people the last thing they would want to see in church is a smile, especially when receiving Communion. If Leon Bloy is correct, however, the eucharist is the ultimate joyful mystery and, as eucharistic ministers we should be signs and carriers of eucharistic joy.

What is eucharistic joy? Recall that "eucharist" comes from a Greek word that means "thanksgiving." As eucharistic ministers we are called to be thankful people, people so aware of how much we have to be thankful for that we carry a tangible, if quiet sense of joy to all those to whom we give Communion, whether in church or on home or hospital visits. Far from being carriers of grim solemnity, as eucharistic ministers we offer ourselves as instruments of the deep joy that only the eucharist can nourish—even for those who are sick or dying.

G. K. Chesterton, an early 20th-century English convert to Catholicism and a deeply joyful man himself, concluded his classic, *Orthodoxy,* with these words: "There was some one thing that was too great for God to show us when He walked upon our earth; and I have sometimes fancied that it was His mirth."

The eucharist is a joyful mystery. It is the joyful mystery of the Resurrection present in the whole person of the risen Christ. When we bring Communion to someone we bring to him or her the Christ we sing about in the old Shaker hymn: "Dance, dance, wherever you may be. / I am the Lord of the Dance said he." We bring the joy of the risen Christ in the eucharist and the joy of the risen Christ at the heart of the universe.

In his modern classic, *New Seeds of Contemplation,* Thomas Merton wrote that God invites us "to forget ourselves on purpose, cast our awful solemnity to the winds and join in the general dance."

When we receive Communion, and when we as eucharistic ministers bring Communion to others, by that fact, in our heart, we "forget ourselves on purpose, cast our awful solemnity to the winds and join in the general dance." For in the eucharist we receive not only the risen Christ present to us now, we also receive the grace of eternal life while still thrashing about in time and space. Is this not cause for joy?

No matter how ordinary or how solemn the circumstances, as eucharistic ministers we come into the presence of those to whom we bring Communion with a special light in our eyes, the light of the risen Christ, the light of the joyful mystery that is the eucharist.

For I am not ashamed
of the gospel;
it is the power of God
for salvation to everyone
who has faith. . .

ROMANS 1:16

Chapter 2

The Faith of
the Eucharistic Minister

MORE THAN A FEW PEOPLE have a wacky idea of faith. Some think that faith means believing in some thing "out there." The thing "out there" people think faith refers to is, of course, "God." For such people, faith means accepting the existence of a Supreme Being "out there," indeed, "WAY out there," beyond the stars, beyond the cosmos, farther than that even. Infinitely far.

Dr. Seuss, author of *The Cat in the Hat, The 500 Hats of Bartholomew Cubbins,* and other modern classics for children and the young at heart, once wrote a prayer. This prayer clearly echoes the "belief-in-a-Supreme-Being-way-out-there" concept of faith. "A Child's Prayer," by Dr. Seuss, begins like this:

> From here on earth,
> From my small place
> I ask of You
> Way out in space. . .

In a sense, Dr. Seuss' prayer is appropriate because it reflects a childish notion of both God and faith. The Catholic understanding of faith is quite different. Catholics are uncomfortable with the "Supreme Being" idea of God, and Catholics do not think that God is "way out in space"—although He is there, too, of course. Rather, the most basic Catholic understanding of God comes from Jesus—God's most complete self-revelation in human history—who teaches us that God is first and foremost our Abba. Typically, translators render this Aramaic word as "Father," but a more accurate translation would be "loving Papa."

Granted, no less a theologian than St. Thomas Aquinas in the thirteenth century insisted that the first thing we must say about God is that we can say nothing. God is the ultimate mystery, far outstripping the capacity of the human intellect to comprehend. Once we acknowledge this, however, St. Thomas said, then we may, and should, make our feeble human efforts to express who God is for us. This is where Jesus comes in, and he teaches us to call God our "loving Papa." It's as if Jesus said, "The best I can do to explain the Divine Mystery is to use the metaphor of a loving Papa."

Yes, God is incomprehensible. So we go with the best metaphor we have, and that is "loving

Papa," and this metaphor is more accurate than inaccurate. The mystery is, therefore, not over-whelming, not radically fearful. Rather, God is love, unconditional, completely reliable, totally trustworthy love. Not only that, but our God is not "way out in space." Our God is, as St. Augustine declared fifteen hundred years ago, closer to us than we are to ourselves.

This is the God of Catholicism, not "way out in space," but a loving Papa who is closer to us than we are to ourselves. Indeed, Father Karl Rahner, S.J., probably the greatest Catholic theo-logian of the twentieth century summed up his entire theology with the phrase, "God lives in you." That is how close our God is to us—not "way out in space," but "in you."

For Catholicism, faith is not believing in some thing, it is knowing Someone—God our loving Papa and Jesus God's Son, the risen Christ who lives in us and in our midst as a community of his disciples. In other words, for Catholicism, faith is most basically a *personal relationship*, not a "head trip;" a personal relationship, not belief in some thing because "the Bible," or "the Church" said so. Faith is loving intimacy with God and with the risen Christ. Here and now. Now and here.

All this is true. At the same time, something

from the opposite direction is equally true. As eucharistic ministers, we bring to our ministry the risen Christ for people to consume to nourish their souls and bodies. The eucharist is about intimacy with the divine in the midst of the human. But as close as the risen Christ comes to us in Holy Communion, something much bigger happens, too, something *Much* Bigger.

In *Teaching a Stone to Talk,* Annie Dillard, a Pulitzer Prize-winning author and convert to Catholicism writes:

> Why do we people in churches seem like cheerful, brainless tourists on a packaged tour of the Absolute? . . . .
>
> On the whole, I do not find Christians, outside of the catacombs, sufficiently sensible of conditions. Does anyone have the foggiest idea what sort of power we so blithely invoke? Or, as I suspect, does no one believe a word of it? The churches are children playing on the floor with their chemistry sets, mixing up a batch of TNT to kill a Sunday morning. It is madness to wear ladies' straw hats and velvet hats to church; we should all be wearing crash helmets. Ushers should issue life preservers and signal flares; they should lash us to our pews.

Eucharistic ministers, of all people, would do well to cultivate both Annie Dillard's sense of humor and her sense of the earth-shaking nature of what we are about. Sometimes to observe a typical Sunday morning or Saturday evening congregation you would think that, indeed, no one believes a word of it. It's all play acting, everyone seems so blasé. Oh, it happens every day, you know, this business of the risen Christ, the Lord of the universe, becoming present under the appearances of bread and wine so we can pop him into our mouths and swallow him. Ho-hum. No big deal.

We would do well to get a grip, now and then, and think about what we are up to. The faith of a eucharistic minister should be a both/and kind of faith. It should blend the intimacy of the eucharist with a deep perception of the holiness, the earth-shaking sacredness of the eucharist. In Holy Communion the risen Christ gives himself to us as our nourishment. As close as husband and wife are to each other when they make love, the intimacy of Christ with his people in the eucharist is closer.

At the same time, the eucharist is an event that, in the spiritual sphere, constitutes an overwhelming explosion. Annie Dillard's metaphors of crash helmets, life preservers, signal flares, and being lashed to our pews are perfectly appropriate. When we gather for the eucharist, surely someone should advise us to buckle our seat belts and hang on. Boring or dull is the last thing the eucharist should be, even—perhaps especially—when the liturgy is done with solemnity.

Then again, it is also true that a eucharistic faith is about more than the eucharist itself. When we celebrate the eucharist we celebrate the faith—the loving intimacy with God and with His people—that we strive to live out on a daily basis. Therefore, a eucharistic faith is as everyday as you can get. In fact, it is the daily attempt to live our faith that gives the deepest meaning to the eucharist. If we are not trying to live our faith every day, participation in the eucharist on Sunday begins to seem senseless. On the other hand, we celebrate the eucharist to nourish our everyday faith.

English mystery writer P. D. James, in her novel *The Black Tower,* has a character named Father Baddeley drop this perfect little observation: "But this is the spiritual life; the ordinary things that one does from day to day."

In the eucharist we find the ultimate union of the holy and the ordinary. As Catholics, we find the holy in the ordinary because that is what the Incarnation was and is, the ultimate union of holy and ordinary, of divinity and humanity. So our eucharistic faith is a faith constantly conditioned by this same union, the perfect transformation of ordinary bread and wine into the whole person of the risen Christ. This is the heart of a eucharistic faith and a eucharistic spirituality in the knock-about world.

Is there anything utterly unique about the faith of a eucharistic minister, anything that makes our faith different from the faith of Catholics who are not eucharistic ministers? The answer is no. Absolutely, no. And yes. Positively, yes. The faith of a eucharistic minister is the same faith shared by the whole church. The fact that one is a eucharistic minister does not change that.

At the same time, just as every human relationship is unique because it involves unique individuals, so each person's faith is unique because each person is unique and relates to God as his or her own unique self. Add to that being a eucharistic minister, and we must conclude that each eucharistic minister's faith is unique because each one has a unique relationship with the eucharist.

It is your own unique person and faith that you bring to your role as a eucharistic minister. It is just as important to be your own unique self, and be in touch with your own faith, as it is to do what all eucharistic ministers do. Be in touch with the risen Christ present in your unique life. Be sensitive to the special ways you may feel called to be of service. Be aware that the time may come when you may be invited to do something special, to go the extra mile, for the sake of your faith, for love of neighbor, in order to do what you as a unique eucharistic minister can do.

If a eucharistic minister has a special gift to bring to the world, perhaps it will be a special awareness of the risen Christ present in his or her own heart at all times, and present in the deepest center of other people at all times.

This chapter began with the observation that sometimes people have wacky ideas of faith. Another wacky idea of faith would say that faith is incompatible with questions and uncertainty. Such an idea of faith is the flip side of the wacky notion that authentic faith is identical with "blind faith." Just as real faith is anything but blind, real faith is not only compatible with questions and uncertainty, it is inseparable from them. Real faith asks questions and knows lack of certainty. This is true of a eucharistic faith in a particular way.

Sometimes eucharistic ministers have questions that, in the old days, priests were more likely to ask than lay folk. Being so close to the eucharistic elements, the bread and the wine faith tells us are now the whole person of the risen Christ, can lead to questions because of how familiar we become with them. To regularly handle hosts and consecrated wine reinforces that what we hold surely appears to be nothing more than wafers of bread, surely appears to be just wine. We may find ourselves puzzling over the mystery. How can this little wafer of bread be the whole person of the risen Christ? How can what appears to be wine be the body and blood, soul and divinity of the risen Lord Jesus?

The faith of Catholics, and in particular the faith of a eucharistic minister, is not afraid to ask such questions, to look such questions straight in the eye. We should not be afraid of such questions because to face them and search for some answers can only increase our faith, deepen the mystery, and lead us into a more prayerful attitude with regard to the eucharist.

What seems, for all the world, to be ordinary wafers of bread and ordinary wine, are in reality Something Else Entirely. How can this be? This is the same question people have asked ever since Jesus insisted that he would give his flesh to eat and his blood to drink. (See John 6:52.) It is a question worth asking, but only faith—personal intimacy with Christ—has an answer, an answer only the heart can hear.

How can this ordinary looking man be the Son of God? Only faith, a personal encounter leading to a personal relationship with him can answer that question. Once that personal relationship exists, there is no clear scientific answer to the question. The question continues to float on the level of the intellect, but the heart whispers to the intellect, "Don't worry about it. Love is the only answer. Nothing can be proved, and nothing can be disproved. Love is all."

> "There is a boy here who has five barley loaves and two fish. But what are they among so many people?"
> Jesus said, "Make the people sit down." Now there was a great deal of grass in the place; so they sat down, about five thousand in all. Then Jesus took the loaves, and when he had given thanks, he distributed them to those who were seated; so also the fish, as much as they wanted (John 6:9-11).

How did Jesus share five loaves of barley bread and two fishy fish so five thousand people could stuff themselves? Endless speculation about figurative language and metaphors to the contrary, we do not know, but we know that he did. How does Jesus share with us the mystery of his risen self looking like bread and wine? We do not know, but we know that he does. The questions do not go away, but they cease to be important most of the time.

Now and then, of course, from time to time, it's good to grab a book on the eucharist, to read some understandable theology in order to increase our understanding of a mystery we will never understand completely. (See Resources at the end of this book.) To say that the eucharist is a "mystery" is not a way to cultivate anti-intellectualism. It is a way to awaken the heart.

The faith of a eucharistic minister can grow and deepen in many ways, not the least of which is by reading poetry. Indeed, it is good for a eucharistic minister to have the heart of a poet for the eucharist itself bears a kinship to poetry in more ways than one. Just as poetry packs Meaning, Beauty, Insight, Humor, and So Forth, into a string of ordinary words, so the eucharist packs divine life into ordinary bread and wine.

Take a delightful poem by Native American Catholic poet Sherman Alexie, a poem in his book *The Summer of Black Widows* (Hanging Loose Press, 1996), from which a eucharistic minister may learn something new about the eucharist. This is an excerpt from Sherman Alexie's poem,

"Drum as Love, Fear, and Prayer":

> Then she tells me Jesus is
> still here
> because Jesus was
> once here
>
> and parts of Jesus are
> still floating in the air.
> She tells me Jesus' DNA is
> part of the collective DNA.
>
> She tells me we are all part
> of Jesus, we are all Jesus
> in part. She tells me to breathe deep
> during all of our storms
>
> because you can sometimes taste Jesus
> in a good, hard rain.

The faith of a eucharistic minister is the faith of the entire church in microcosm. It is one person intimately related to the risen Christ as the whole church is related to the risen Christ. That is the mystery at the heart of what a eucharistic minister is about, is up to, is doing. Keep this secret in your pocket like a coin. Keep this secret in your heart.

In his posthumously published book, *A Vow*

of Conversation: Journals 1964-1965 (Farrar, Straus, Giroux, 1988), Thomas Merton wrote some words that ring like a bell for a eucharistic minister. Merton wrote on January 6, 1965:

> . . . I went down to the spring, found it without trouble. Wonderful clear water pouring strongly out of the cleft in the mossy rock. I drank from it in my cupped hands and suddenly realized it was years, perhaps twenty-five or thirty years, since I had tasted such water. Absolutely pure and clear and sweet with the freshness of untouched water. No chemicals.
>
> I looked up at the clear sky and the tops of the leafless trees shining in the sun and it was a moment of angelic lucidity. I said the Psalms of Tierce with great joy, overflowing joy, as if the land and woods and spring were all praising God through me. Again the sense of angelic transparency of everything: of pure, simple and total light.

These moments Merton described are as eucharistic as they can be, in a pure, pristine way. They are eucharistic because they evoke the holy in the midst of the ordinary, the sacred in the midst of creation, which is what the eucharist is—

the holy, smack, dead center, in the middle of our ordinary lives. Ideally, one thing the eucharist should do for our faith is enable us to recognize the holy in the ordinary more often. With Merton, as eucharistic ministers we should "specialize" in seeing God everywhere and allowing all of creation to praise God through us.

In the long run, and in the short run, faith depends on being eucharistic in all that we do— that is, it depends on being a thankful, thankful person. In his song, "Botswanna," singer/song writer John Stewart sings, "Oh faith it is a fire, / And it's fanned by the winds of thanks." This is what it means to have a eucharistic faith, to fan the fire of faith with the winds of thanks.

The faith of a eucharistic minister is a faith that finds endless reasons to give thanks. "And whatever you do, in word or deed," says the Letter to the Colossians, "do everything in the name of the Lord Jesus, giving thanks to God the Father through him" (3:17). Notice, the author of Colossians does not say that we are to give thanks only when things go the way we want them to go, only when life is a bowl of cherries. He simply says that we are to do everything in the name of the Lord Jesus and give thanks to God. These are important words for a eucharistic minister, whose entire spirituality is based on *eucharistia*, giving thanks.

When you are sick, be sick in the name of the Lord Jesus, and give thanks as you try to recover. When you are well, be well in the name of the Lord Jesus, and give thanks as you go about your day. When you are unemployed, be unemployed in the name of the Lord Jesus, and give thanks while you look for work. When your plans fall through, be disappointed in the name of the Lord Jesus, and give thanks as you make other plans. All things here below carry a blessing, that is the point. All things carry a blessing if we are open to the blessing and ready to receive it. When we give thanks in the midst of "whatever" we acknowledge this blessing and announce our readiness to receive it.

We find it easy to complain, of course; we find it easy to moan and whine even in our prayer. Maybe especially in our prayer. Self-pity is almost a national pastime. A eucharistic faith, on the contrary, is a faith that seeks the blessing in anything and everything and gives thanks even before seeing or knowing what the blessing is. This, at least, is the ideal for which a eucharistic minister strives.

May the God of hope
fill you with all joy and peace
in believing,
so that you may abound in hope
by the power of the Holy Spirit.

ROMANS 15:13

Chapter 3

The Hope of
the Eucharistic Minister

HOPE, O MY SOUL, hope. You know neither the day nor the hour. Watch carefully, for everything passes quickly, even though your impatience makes doubtful what is certain, and turns a very short time into a long one. Dream that the more you struggle, the more you prove the love that you bear your God, and the more you will rejoice one day with your Beloved, in a happiness and rapture that can never end.

ST. TERESA OF AVILA

Listen not only with your ears, but with your heart. Listen.

Hope, like faith, is one of what are traditionally called the three "theological virtues," the third being charity, or love—to which we will turn in Chapter 4. Faith, hope, and charity are "theological" virtues because they have to do with our direct relationship with God. In all three cases, however, each virtue has profound implications for our relationships with other people, as well. For as we saw in the chapter on faith, we cannot separate our relationship with God from our relationships with other people.

It is particularly appropriate to speak of hope in the life of a eucharistic minister, for the eucharist nourishes hope in a particular way. When we celebrate the eucharist we recreate the last supper Jesus shared with his disciples. At the same time, the eucharist is an experience of the future breaking into our lives in the present. We experience the beginnings, even now, of the grace of resurrection because in the eucharist we share in the Resurrection of Christ to whom we are joined by baptism. The eucharist nourishes hope by giving us the grace of our own future resurrection, and what better cause for hope than this?

When a faith community gathers for Mass it celebrates faith, hope, and charity as a way of life. Believers gather to worship not one another but God—an important point in an era when the common ecclesiology or theology of the church and its resulting liturgies, and even the architecture of church interiors, sometimes seem to suggest the worshiping community turned in on itself. Obviously, relationships with one another are important, but it is our faith—our shared relationship with the risen Christ—that gathers us together for liturgy; then our shared worship nourishes our life as a parish and as a church.

Hang on, now. Out of necessity, this is going to get rather abstract. Recall that when we receive Holy Communion we receive the whole person of the risen Christ. Therefore, we eat and drink our ultimate destiny. The Resurrection of Christ nourishes us here and now, and at the same time we are nourished by that eternal life for which we are destined to have a full share as members of the body of Christ. Thus, in the eucharist we celebrate and nourish hope, hope not just for this life but for eternal life.

How's that for a mind stretcher? As eucharistic ministers we share with others the body and blood of the risen Christ, the food of eternal life. Therefore, we share hope, and we nourish hope, both for this life and the next. Suddenly, some words of St. Paul take on new depth of meaning: "For in hope we were saved. Now hope that is seen is not hope. For who hopes for what is seen? But if we hope for what we do not see, we wait for it with patience" (Romans 8:24-25).

"I'll tell you something." The speaker is a man in his mid-sixties who is a eucharistic minister for a parish in Ohio. "When I take Communion to someone who is really sick, or someone who is dying, that's a very profound experience for me. I pray for a few minutes before I go in there, and I pray again after I leave, out there in my car. It's a tremendously moving experience. These people, they receive Communion like it was the best thing that could ever happen to them. Sometimes they cry it makes them so happy. They have hope again, which was growing weaker before they received Communion. They don't have this ho-hum, lackadaisical attitude people often seem to have when they receive Communion in church. People who are sick or dying, they know what the eucharist is all about. I've learned a lot from them."

Hope is remarkable, even astonishing, when it is real. Hope is not mere optimism. Hope is not a simple matter of all the time, psychologically or emotionally, trying to walk on the sunny side of the street. "As long as matters are really hopeful," said G. K. Chesterton (1874-1936), "hope is a mere flattery or platitude; it is only when everything is hopeless that hope begins to be a strength at all."

Hope can, and should, exist under any circumstances, of course. But hope is most recognizable, and attains its deepest reality, when life looks most bleak. "You can survive the darkest night," vocalizes John Stewart, "remembering the sun." It is in the darkest of nights that hope can shine the brightest. This is why it is in people who are very sick or dying that we see most clearly the power of the eucharist to nourish hope.

When we are sick or dying, we gather hope from the eucharist when life seems most hopeless. We gather hope, and the new life that hope gives comes from a sacramental ritual that seems to the unbeliever to be pious whistling in the dark. A few words. A little bread. A splash of wine. But the words, and the bread, and the wine are but the surface appearances of the Reality they carry, a Reality only Christian faith—loving intimacy with God in Christ—can perceive.

A few words, a little bread, a splash of wine: to the person with little or no experience of loving intimacy with a loving God they are hardly anything at all. But the words, and the bread, and the wine, no longer mere words, no longer just bread and wine, mysteriously they carry the Love that makes the cosmos spin and sparkle in an orderly fashion, the Love that keeps life pulsing in our hearts now and forever, world without end, in this life and the next.

When we bring Holy Communion to someone who is sick or dying, we share with that person the knowledge that comes from authentic hope. Eighteenth-century English poet, artist and mystic William Blake said it as well as anyone. He said that to die is simply to pass from one room to another, and Blake himself died singing—literally. When we bring Holy Communion, we bring this knowledge, something of this lightness of spirit, which nourishes hope of the most real kind, a hope that goes beyond this life. This is the deepest dimension of our eucharistic ministry.

At the same time, of course, most of the time we share Holy Communion with someone he or she is neither sick nor dying. We give Communion to ordinary people in the midst of their ordinary lives. The people to whom we give Communion are respectful enough, yet they may seem to have that "lackadaisical" attitude the eucharistic minister from Ohio remarked upon. Don't jump to conclusions too quickly, however.

As a eucharistic minister it is good to cultivate the ability to look beneath the surface, to move beyond a superficial perspective, especially when it comes to other people. The people who line up to receive Communion during Mass may seem to be, shall we say, respectfully nonchalant. They shuffle through the Communion line, and when they get to you they extend their hands or tongue for Communion. Maybe they step to the side and bless themselves with the sign of the cross. Then they return to their pews. It may all seem rather ordinary. But don't be fooled.

Who is this ordinary looking person who shuffles up, extends hands or tongue for Communion, and shuffles away again? This is a person who at least some of the time, perhaps much of the time, struggles with hopelessness. He or she has more than a fair share of anguish to carry. Who is this person? She is a mother with young children driving her to distraction and another one on the way. He is a father with teenagers who make choices that keep him awake nights, worrying. She is an unemployed woman who doesn't know where her next rent payment is coming from, or if it will come at all. He is the husband of an alcoholic. She seems to have a fairly comfortable life, but her husband never comes with her to church. Who knows what anguish she lives with?

Her mother has cancer. His son has been expelled from high school for drug possession. Her teenage daughter is pregnant. His wife has Alzheimer's disease. Their doctor told them a few days ago that their baby will be born with a genetic defect. He is an alcoholic in denial. She was sexually abused as a child. Here is a man whose teenage son is smoking cigarettes, and he wonders what he did wrong as a father. The list is virtually endless. Large and small, we all have our crosses to carry.

We all have our crosses. As a eucharistic minister, you might imagine all those people in line for Communion as if they carry crosses with them, heavy on their shoulders, dragging them up the aisle as they come for Communion. You can't see their crosses, of course, but they are real, those crosses are there, as surely as God made little green apples and cumquats. Use your imagination. Use the eyes of faith. You will have no trouble believing that each person who approaches you for Holy Communion carries a cross and needs some hope, a little bit of hope to get through the day ahead, the week ahead. They come to Mass, and they come to you to receive Communion, for a "hope transfusion," if you will.

Keep this in mind as you place the great mystery, the whole person of the risen Christ, in each person's hands or on his or her tongue. Keep this in mind as you share the chalice or cup that no longer holds wine but the great mystery, the whole person of the risen Christ. To each one speak the words, "Body of Christ," or "Blood of Christ" not with your lips only. Speak those words from your heart. Try to make eye contact as you speak. Share the Christ in yourself, too. Let the words you speak be a prayer, not just words spoken in rote fashion, over and over, blah, blah, blah. As a eucharistic minister, you are a minister of hope. So give hope by the way you offer to each person the risen Lord Jesus, "body and blood, soul and divinity." Let it be.

The pre-Vatican II Latin Mass, with the approval of the local bishop, is sometimes celebrated in parishes today. In the Latin liturgy, when the priest gives each person Communion he says, *"Corpus Domini nostri Jesu Christi custodiat animam tuam in vitam aeternam. Amen."* Which means: "May the Body of our Lord Jesus Christ keep your soul unto life everlasting. Amen."

In the contemporary vernacular liturgy, of course, the priest or eucharistic minister simply says, "Body of Christ," or "Blood of Christ." All the same, the meaning stated explicitly in the old Latin Mass is inherent in the new abbreviated formula, and the words are words of hope. When you speak these few words, know that your message is a prayer like the prayer spoken in the old Latin formula. The words are fewer, but the prayer is the same.

There is an old English proverb: "If it were not for hope the heart would break." When we say that as eucharistic ministers we are ministers of hope this is to say a great deal. For everyone walks around with a broken heart. Children break the hearts of their parents, parents break the hearts of their children. Husbands and wives break each other's heart. We all have a broken heart. Sooner or later, in one way or another, life is a heart-breaking experience. In this sense, the eucharist gives a hope that heals broken hearts. Indeed, sometimes all that stands between the people to whom we minister and a completely broken heart is the sacrament we offer them, this sacrament that gives them a hope that heals.

Tristan Bernard (1866-1947) was a great French dramatist and novelist. During World War II, Bernard and his wife were interned by the Gestapo. "The time of fear is over," Bernard told his wife when they were arrested. "Now comes the time of hope."

Sometimes we forget that the eucharist is a re-creation of the Passover meal shared by Jesus with his disciples on the brink of his own terrible suffering and death. We forget that in the eucharist, as in the Christian life as a whole, we cannot separate death and resurrection. Yes, in the eucharist we receive the whole person of the risen Christ. But we share, also, in his death on the cross. Just as Jesus shared the sacrament of hope on the verge of what looked like a hopeless situation, so when we celebrate the eucharist we should not expect the result to be life on a spiritual Sunnybrook Farm.

The hope we share as eucharistic ministers is

not a spiritual aspirin designed to cure life's headaches. Rather, when we give Communion to others we offer them the hope and nourishment they need to "keep on keeping on," to maintain life in the midst of whatever each day lays on their doorstep and to do so with at least a modicum of peace and tranquility.

The anecdote about Tristan Bernard is a good illustration of what the eucharist should do for us. It should help us to put fear behind us and live with hope, even when prospects look most bleak. This movement from fear to hope is at the heart of what we do as eucharistic ministers, and it should be at the heart of our self-understanding. When we share Holy Communion during Mass, or when we bring Communion to people outside of Mass, we should intend to help them to be a little less fearful and a little more hopeful. That should be our personal prayer before, during, and after the Communion ritual. A little less fearful, a little more hopeful.

In the Gospels, Jesus admonishes his disciples time after time to put fear behind them and trust in his Father's love. The story of Jesus calming the storm on the lake is, perhaps, the paradigm for all situations in our lives where we become fearful and lose hope:

"One day [Jesus] got into a boat with his disciples, and he said to them, 'Let us go across to the other side of the lake.' So they put out, and while they were sailing he fell asleep. A windstorm swept down on the lake, and the boat was filling with water, and they were in danger. They went to him and woke him up, shouting, 'Master, Master, we are perishing!' And he woke up and rebuked the wind and the raging waves; they ceased, and there was a calm. He said to them, 'Where is your faith?'" (Luke 8:22-25a).

"Do not let your hearts be troubled," Jesus says in John's Gospel, "and do not let them be afraid" (14:27b).

As eucharistic ministers, this ministry of Jesus to banish fear and encourage faith, trust, hope and peace, is our ministry. When we give Holy Communion to others we offer them the ultimate source of hope, the "whole person" of the risen Christ, who nourishes trust and hope.

Let us not underestimate the importance of this ministry of hope. This is not just a pious platitude. We are talking about life itself when we talk about hope, for there is no life where there is no hope. Recall that in Dante's *Inferno*, over the gates of hell hangs a sign: "Abandon hope, all ye who enter here" (III,1.9). From Dante's perspective, hell is the absence of all hope. In a very real sense, therefore, when we share with others the sacrament of hope, the eucharist, we help them to avoid the hell of hopelessness.

Remarkably, it is often the young who have the most difficulty with hope while the middle-aged and the old understand hope and rejoice in it. In *Charles Dickens* (1906), G. K. Chesterton wrote:

> . . .youth is the period in which a man can be hopeless. The end of every episode is the end of the world. But the power of hoping through everything, the knowledge that the soul survives its adventures, that great inspiration comes to the middle-aged; God has kept that good wine until now. It is from the backs of the elderly gentlemen that the wings of the butterfly should burst.

As eucharistic ministers, we may be inclined to have less sympathy, compassion, and understanding for teenagers and young adults than we could. It's relatively easy to give Communion with a smile and a nod of kindness to an older person who, we suppose, needs our encouragement and the grace of the sacrament in a special way. In fact, the oddly dressed and coifed teen-ager may be the one on the verge of despair, so make the extra effort to convey the hope and peace of Christ when he or she receives Communion from your hands.

The hope of the eucharistic minister is the hope of the eucharist itself, which comes from the power of the Resurrection we share when we give Communion to others. Both our faith and our hope, however, are nourished by charity, or love, which is the ultimate Reality at the center of creation and in the deepest center of each and every person, the ultimate Reality in which "we live and move and have our being" (Acts 17:28).

When they had finished breakfast,
Jesus said to Simon Peter,
"Simon son of John, do you love me
more than these?" He said to him,
"Yes, Lord; you know that I love you."
Jesus said to him, "Feed my lambs."
A second time he said to him,
"Simon son of John, do you love me?"
He said to him, "Yes, Lord;
you know that I love you."
Jesus said to him, "Tend my sheep."
He said to him the third time,
"Simon son of John, do you love me?"
Peter felt hurt because he said to him
the third time, "Do you love me?"
And he said to him,
"Lord, you know everything;
you know that I love you."
Jesus said to him, "Feed my sheep."

JOHN 21:15-17

Chapter 4

The Love of
the Eucharistic Minister

"LOVE" IS a wild and wooly word. It is a difficult word to get a grip on because of all the ways people use and misuse it. Frederick Buechner, in his contemporary classic, *Wishful Thinking: A Theological ABC* (Harper & Row, 1973), has some pithy observations about "love":

> To lose yourself in another's arms, or in another's company, or in suffering for all men who suffer, including the ones who inflict suffering upon you—to lose yourself in such ways is to find yourself. Is what it's all about. Is what love is. . . .
>
> In the Christian sense, love is not primarily an emotion but an act of the will. When Jesus tells us to love our neighbors, he is not telling us to love them in the sense of responding to them with a cozy emotional feeling. . . Thus in Jesus' terms we can love our neighbors without necessarily liking

them. In fact liking them may stand in the way of loving them by making us overprotective sentimentalists instead of reasonably honest friends.

The inclination is to cast about for another word to avoid confusion. Time was, "charity" would do, but no more. A contemporary dictionary's first definition of "charity" is: "the provision of help or relief to the poor." Traced to its Latin root, *caritas*, however, charity refers to God's benevolent love for us and likewise our love for one another. This is the love or charity that is the crown jewel of the theological virtues, faith, hope, and love/charity.

This is the love St. Paul has in mind in his famous words from the First Letter to the Corinthians: "And now faith, hope, and love abide, these three; and the greatest of these is love" (13:13). As eucharistic ministers, we are called to love as Jesus loves, of course. But what might this mean in practical terms, specifically in the context of our eucharistic ministry? One thing it does not mean is that we are called to be chummy.

Sometimes eucharistic ministers, particularly when commissioned to lead Communion services in the absence of a priest, take their cues from priests who, for example, begin Mass with "Good morning!" and conclude with "Have a nice day!" The presumption seems to be that "The Lord be with you" and "Go in peace to love and serve the Lord" no longer carry enough meaning for the followers of Christ, so we need to supplement the traditional words with secular platitudes. Sometimes, such priests also sprinkle cheery remarks here and there throughout the Mass, or modify or substitute other prayers for the prayers in the Sacramentary to make the Mass more "natural" or "relevant."

There is nothing more loving about this approach to the Mass or to a Communion service. It may be chummy, but it's not an improved form of worship, and it does not communicate more effectively the love of God. All it does is trivialize the eucharist. Regardless of the specific context, whether helping to distribute Communion during Mass, taking Communion to people unable to attend Mass, or leading a Communion service in the absence of a priest, eucharistic ministers should feel no need to entertain or inspire those to whom they give Holy Communion.

It is not the task of the eucharistic minister to endear himself or herself to others by being chummy, cheerful, full of sunbeams and snappy patter. The ideal is to become "transparent" to the ritual, to serve the ritual and not let your personality get in the way. Simply follow the prescribed ritual, allowing the living tradition and prayers to speak for themselves. No one should presume to be so inspired by God that he or she can improve on the prayers and rituals provided by the church.

For home, hospital, or nursing home visits, there should be a clear demarcation between the "visit" portion of the visit and the Communion ritual portion of the visit. Ritual is not an ad-lib exercise. Ritual is, by definition, the repetition of the same basic prayers and actions for each Communion service. This is the best way to communicate God's love to those we serve and not let our personality—sparkling as it no doubt is—and personal quirks get in the way.

All that said, as eucharistic ministers we are called to be an instrument of God's love to those to who receive Communion from us. Especially when we bring Communion to those who cannot attend Mass, as eucharistic ministers we are more than a delivery service for consecrated hosts. We need to share ourselves with those we visit. Often such people simply need someone who is willing to listen. We may feel inclined to rush in and rush out, but we need to be with each person to whom we bring Communion. Each visit should have four parts: getting in touch with the person we are there for, the Communion service itself, a few minutes of neighborly visiting, and the time to say an informal blessing and goodbye. Of course, the better we know the person to whom we bring Communion, the more informal and unstructured all this will become.

Clearly, being a eucharistic minister is a way to love our neighbors. This is one outstanding example, however, of a situation where we cannot give what we do not have. Sure, we can stand there and hand out Communion to people in the context of the eucharist. If commissioned to do so, we can lead Communion services in the absence of a priest. We can take Communion to those unable to attend Mass. But apart from a rich inner life, a living spirituality, we can do little more than go about our ministry in a mechanical fashion. To exercise our eucharistic ministry fully, we need to do so out of a heart filled with love for God, and this requires time each day for prayer.

We live in an era with a strong inclination to identify love for God with love for neighbor. Pay close attention, however, to the words of Jesus:

> One of the scribes came near and heard them disputing with one another, and seeing that [Jesus] answered them well, he asked him, "Which commandment is the

first of all?" Jesus answered, "The first is, 'Hear, O Israel: the Lord our God, the Lord is one; you shall love the Lord your God with all your heart, and with all your soul, and with all your mind, and with all your strength.' The second is this, 'You shall love your neighbor as yourself.' There is no other commandment greater than these" (Mark 12:28-31).

Jesus insists that love of neighbor is basic and indispensable, but he is equally clear that his disciples are to love God for His own sake. We cannot simply go about "doing good" for other people and claim to be followers of Christ. A humanistic atheist can do as much. We need to be prayerful people, as well, and as eucharistic ministers our prayer is fundamental to our eucharistic ministry.

The prayer life of any Catholic can be divided into three kinds: liturgical and paraliturgical prayer, private prayer, and informal group prayer. For a eucharistic minister, it is particularly appropriate to participate in the eucharist as frequently as possible. If work schedules allow, participation in daily Mass is an excellent habit to cultivate. Once you begin attending daily Mass, after two or three weeks you will find that your day seems incomplete if for some reason you cannot attend Mass and receive Holy Communion.

In his first encyclical, *Redemptor Hominis* (1979), Pope John Paul II wrote:

> The Church never ceases to relive [Jesus'] death on the Cross and his Resurrection, which constitute the content of the Church's daily life. Indeed, it is by the command of Christ himself, her Master, that the Church unceasingly celebrates the Eucharist, finding in it the "fountain of life and holiness" [see the Litany of the Sacred Heart], the efficacious sign of grace and reconciliation with God, and the pledge of eternal life (7.4).

These words sum up beautifully why the habit of attending daily eucharist is so beneficial. Our entire life, as Christians and as eucharistic ministers, is a participation in the Cross and Resurrection of Jesus. In virtue of our baptism we share in this mystery at the heart of the Christian life. To attend Mass and receive Communion frequently is to nourish ourselves with the sacrament of our unity with the Cross and Resurrection of Christ. The Mass nourishes us with the word of God in the scriptures and with the whole person of the risen Christ in Holy Communion.

There simply is no more beneficial form of prayer for any Catholic, and for a eucharistic minister in particular, whose ministry is focused on the eucharist.

Closely related to the eucharist are eucharistic devotions. As eucharistic ministers we may find these devotions of special value for nourishing a eucharistic spirituality. Traditional eucharistic devotions include simple "visits" to the Blessed Sacrament in a parish church, as well as Benediction, Exposition, and Adoration of the Blessed Sacrament. Following the Second Vatican Council, in the mid-1960s, eucharistic devotions such as these fell into disfavor. A perfectly justifiable concern for placing the Mass in the center of the church's life led to neglect of the old eucharistic devotions. In the early 1990s, however, Catholics began to rediscover the value of these "old-fashioned" devotional practices.

When the words and actions of Christ are repeated by a priest, the bread and wine of the eucharist, in a mysterious but real way, become the whole person, "body and blood, soul and divinity," of the risen Christ. It was only logical that in the early church this fact would lead to worship of the eucharistic elements both within and outside of the eucharistic celebration.

Father Benedict Groeschel, C.F.R., and James

Monti, in their book *In the Presence of Our Lord: The History, Theology, and Psychology of Eucharistic Devotion* (Our Sunday Visitor Books, 1997), present a historical overview. They explain that by the second century the consecrated bread—now the whole person of the risen Christ—was kept after Mass concluded so that it might be taken to those who were sick or in prison. Soon the consecrated bread was kept in a locked place in the sacristy of the church, and by the first half of the fifth century the sacrament had been moved to a tabernacle on the altar of at least some churches. By the tenth century, this was common practice.

Adoration of the Blessed Sacrament is a devotional practice much to be recommended for eucharistic ministers. Time spent prayerfully in the presence of the Blessed Sacrament nourishes a eucharistic spirituality and helps cultivate a deeper devotion to and respect for the Mass and for Holy Communion. The eucharistic minister who makes regular prayerful "visits" to the Blessed Sacrament, and/or regularly spends time in prayer before the exposed sacrament—in a chapel of Perpetual Adoration, for example—is a eucharistic minister who will carry a more lively spirit of love for the eucharist to those who receive Communion from him or her.

A word of clarification about eucharistic

devotions. The value of eucharistic devotions comes from the fact that they are inseparable from the Mass itself. Eucharistic devotions should follow from and lead us back to the Mass. When we worship the risen Christ present in the tabernacle or in a host exposed in a monstrance on the altar of a church or chapel, we do so in union with the celebration of the eucharist at that moment in countless places the world over.

We also worship the eucharistic Christ who is present in many other places—in our families, in our workplaces, and in the grandeur of creation. One of the purposes of eucharistic adoration is to sensitize ourselves to recognize Christ in the people, places, and situations we encounter in our everyday lives. Eucharistic devotions remind us that the Mass is the "summit and source" of our life as a people of faith. Eucharistic devotions help to nourish in us a eucharistic spirit so that we might be eucharistic people in every dimension of our lives.

Eucharistic devotions have their place. These devotions can, and should, be given a clear scriptural character. Those who use such devotions to promote Catholic political or ideological causes misunderstand both the eucharist and eucharistic devotions.

Eucharistic devotions need to retain their connections with the eucharist itself and with the nature and purpose of the eucharist as a communal form of worship. They should also echo a respect for contemplative spirituality which they certainly nourish. One of the main purposes of eucharistic devotions is to nourish a deep sense of how close Christ is to his people and to their everyday lives. Indeed, if anyone cared to do so it would be easy to put together a collection of devotional prayers and scriptural meditations relating significant issues of our time to the eucharistic presence of Christ—issues such as world hunger, poverty, war and peace, respect for life, economic justice, ecumenism, and church renewal.

Note, too, that love for the eucharist, and for the risen Christ mysteriously but really and truly present in the consecrated bread and wine, is the same love upon which the Gospel of John offers an extended meditation. Here scripture and sacrament come together to illumine each other in a way that can only enrich our understanding of what we are about as eucharistic ministers.

In Chapters 13 and 15 of John's Gospel, Jesus says:

I give you a new commandment, that you love one another. Just as I have loved you, you also should love one another. By this everyone will know that you are my disciples, if you have love for one another....

This is my commandment, that you love one another as I have loved you. No one has greater love than this, to lay down one's life for one's friends (13:34-35 & 15:12-13).

Clearly, there is more to love than warm feelings. The Jesus of the Fourth Gospel commands his disciples to love one another—which means to will and actively work for one another's good—but he also insists that our love for one another needs to mirror his love for us. Jesus then explains that he loves us by giving his life for us. This is the same love we are to base our lives, and our eucharistic ministry, upon.

Back up a few chapters in the Gospel of John, however, and we learn even more about Jesus' love for us as a model of our love for one another. Chapter 6 includes, of course, Jesus' bread of life discourse:

The Jews then disputed among themselves, saying, "How can this man give us his flesh to eat?

So Jesus said to them, "Very truly, I tell

you, unless you eat the flesh of the Son of Man and drink his blood, you have no life in you. Those who eat my flesh and drink my blood have eternal life, and I will raise them up on the last day; for my flesh is true food and my blood is true drink. Those who eat my flesh and drink my blood abide in me, and I in them. Just as the living Father sent me, and I live because of the Father, so whoever eats me will live because of me" (6:52-57).

Jesus shows his love for his disciples, and for us, not with words alone but with the gift of himself. This is the tip-off for us to know that as Jesus' disciples we are to love others by giving ourselves to others in service, not just in our eucharistic ministry but in every dimension of daily life. By sharing himself with us the risen Christ gives us the gift of eternal life, and when we give ourselves to others, in our eucharistic ministry and in all the ways we serve others, we share with them the gift of God's love which is also the gift of eternal life.

Here are some words from *The Imitation of Christ*, by Thomas à Kempis (translation by Betty I. Knott, Collins/Fontana Books, 1963), often called the most-read book after the Bible:

Lord, I come to you with all the sincerity of my heart, and with good firm faith; I come with hope and reverence, because you have commanded it, and I really believe that you are present here in the Sacrament, both God and man.

It is your wish that I should receive you and become one with you in love. I therefore pray you for your mercy, and beg you to grant me special grace, so that I may melt away in love and be absorbed in you, no more concerned for any outside comfort. For this Sacrament is most high and most worthy. It is the health of soul and body, the remedy for every sickness of the spirit. By it my faults are cured, my passions curbed, temptations overcome or weakened. Grace is outpoured in richer measure, virtue that has taken root is strengthened; faith is increased, hope made strong, love kindled to envelop all my being (Bk.4, IV).

These words from a great devotional classic remind us that the heart of a eucharistic minister's love is his or her love for Christ in the eucharist. Apart from this love for Christ even the term "eucharist" ("to give thanks"), makes little sense. For ultimately it is Christ himself that we give thanks for, and in particular we give thanks for his gift of himself to us "under the appearances of bread and wine."

Finally, at the risk of sounding merely trendy, it is important for a eucharistic minister to grasp with both hands the truth that no one can love others who does not love self. The point is not to encourage narcissism or egocentric coddling of the self. The point is to appreciate and love yourself as a gift of God sent into the world to be with and for others, a carrier of gifts from God that only you can give. In his little book, *Let Yourself Be Loved* (Paulist Press, 1997), pastoral psychotherapist Phillip Bennett recalls a Hasidic saying: "A host of angels goes in a vanguard before every human being crying out, 'Make way! Make way for the image of God!'"

We need to love ourselves because God loves us. We need to love ourselves rightly if we are to carry out our eucharistic ministry in ways that benefit others in ways they really need. How are we to love ourselves, practically speaking? It's not difficult, especially in our frazzled era. We can love ourselves by being good to ourselves, by maintaining a healthy diet, by getting some exercise regularly, and by taking the time we need for prayer and to continue to learn. We can take the time to read a book, and we can take the time to make a retreat. We can take a day off, and we can take a good long soak in the tub. When we love ourselves in such ways our eucharistic ministry will thrive and truly benefit those we are called to serve.

So now, Father,
glorify me in your own presence
with the glory that I had
in your presence
before the world existed.

JOHN 17:5

Chapter 5

The Presence of
the Eucharistic Minister

NOW WE APPROACH a much neglected dimension of what the eucharistic minister is about. Here it is. The mystery at the heart of the eucharist and at the heart of what we do as eucharistic ministers is a mystery of presence—the real presence of the risen Christ in the eucharist, of course. But we also refer to the real presence of Christ in the eucharistic minister and in those to whom we offer Holy Communion. There is a deep mystery of love at work here, a mystery of divine presence that rarely gets the attention it deserves.

The notion of "presence" occurs over and over in both the Hebrew and Christian Scriptures. In Genesis, after Adam and Eve disobey God, we read: "They heard the sound of the LORD God walking in the garden at the time of the evening breeze, and the man and his wife hid themselves from *the presence of the LORD God* among the trees of the garden" (3:8; emphasis added).

Genesis does not say that Adam and Eve hid themselves from God. Rather, they "hid themselves from *the presence of the LORD God.*" There is something much more personal and intimate about "presence." The couple's sinful condition drives them to hide themselves not just from God but from His "presence."

In the Book of Exodus, this notion of "presence" takes on an even more powerful meaning. By analogy, we may see here a prototype of the eucharistic bread Jesus would give to his people, the church. While Moses is on Mount Sinai, God instructs him, in detail, about how the people of Israel are to worship Him. Prominent among these instructions are these words: "And you shall set the bread of the Presence on the table before me always" (25:30). The "bread of the Presence" was bread placed before God every sabbath as a sacrificial offering and subsequently eaten by the priests.

Later, God tells Moses, "My presence will go with you, and I will give you rest" (Exodus 33:14). Evidently, then, God's "presence" is a personal concept, one meant to not only inspire worship, but one from which we are to draw comfort and consolation.

The First Book of Chronicles says: "Seek the LORD and his strength, seek his presence continually" (16:11). Notice, we are not told to "seek the LORD" only, but to "seek his presence." There is something important about the personal presence of God, something deeper, richer, and more meaningful.

Echoing this line from 1 Chronicles, the Psalmist sings: "Seek the LORD and his strength; seek his presence continually" (105:4).

In the New Testament, in the Gospel of Luke, the angel identifies himself to Mary thus: "I am Gabriel. I stand in the presence of God. . ." (1:19). Again, the angel does not simply say that he stands near God, or next to God, or someplace in the vicinity of God. Rather, he stands "in the presence of God." God's *presence* is personal, it almost seems to have a reality all its own, as if God is too overwhelming, but God's "presence" is something both angels and humans can enter and experience.

In the Gospel of John, Nicodemus comes to Jesus "by night" and says: "Rabbi, we know that you are a teacher who has come from God; for no one can do these signs that you do apart from the presence of God" (3:2). The Fourth Gospel places great emphasis on the divinity of Jesus, and this is one way to accomplish this, by having Nicodemus acknowledge that Jesus of Nazareth is in God's "presence" even prior to his death and

Resurrection. This explains why Jesus is able to "do these signs."

In the Acts of the Apostles, Cornelius tells Peter that "a man in dazzling clothes" appeared and told him to send for Peter. Cornelius concludes: "So now all of us are here in the presence of God to listen to all that the Lord has commanded you to say" (10:33).

Following this encounter with the messenger from God, probably an angel, Cornelius understands that his meeting with Peter, and the gathering of all those present, is "in the presence of God." Luke, the author of the Acts of the Apostles, knows that when the community assembles it does so not just to talk, think, or preach *about* God. Rather, the community gathers "in the presence of God," this very personal, real notion of how close God is to us.

This idea of God's presence extends, as well, to ministry. When we act on behalf of Christ, for others, we do so in union with the personal presence of God. "For we are not peddlers of God's word like so many," says Saint Paul; "but in Christ we speak as persons of sincerity, as persons sent from God and standing in his presence" (2 Cor 2:17).

From this we gather valuable insights into what we are about as eucharistic ministers. We offer people the whole person of the risen Christ, mysteriously yet truly present in Holy Communion. But we bring with us, on an even more fundamental level, the divine presence. As eucharistic ministers, we are "persons sent from God and standing in his presence."

Everything said in the earlier chapters of this book comes into play here and has a reality of its own within this concept of the divine presence. As eucharistic ministers, we stand in God's presence and bring that presence to our ministry, and the characteristics of this presence are joy, faith, hope, and love.

Each eucharistic minister is a unique individual, of course, so each one will bring the divine presence in a unique manner. In his or her own way, each eucharistic minister brings to this ministry a sense of joy at sharing the great mystery of the eucharist. Even when the eucharistic minister brings Holy Communion into a situation where there is illness or the anticipation of death, this deep joy will underlie his or her desire to bring comfort, healing and consolation. For the joy of the eucharist is a joy that is deeper than any sadness, far deeper than any superficial cheeriness, and the eucharist carries the promise of eternal life.

Our presence as eucharistic ministers brings

joy because where the risen Christ is, there is joy. Because we bring the eucharist to others, we cannot help but bring joy simply by being there. For with our presence we bring the presence of the risen Christ. Yet this joy is not mere upbeat optimism. The joy that comes from the eucharist, and the joy that characterizes the presence of the eucharistic minister is a deep joy that remains firmly rooted even in the bleakest of circumstances. It is the joy saints have known as they faced martyrdom for their faith. It is the joy ordinary Christians know as they remain faithful to their commitments when the future looks dark. "Those aren't clouds on the horizon," sings John Stewart, "they're the shadows of the angels' wings."

That said, we may all the same ponder some words spoken by Pope John Paul II: "There is no law which lays it down that you must smile! But you can make a gift of your smile. . ."

Someone once said that, "A grim Catholic is *a grim Catholic.*" Even on solemn or serious occasions, there should be nothing grim about the actions or demeanor of a eucharistic minister. We are called to be carriers of the joy of Christ, even at the bedside of someone who is sick or dying, and even at a funeral. This does not mean we act silly, like mindless nincompoops, of course, but it does mean that we eschew any suggestion that we are grim about our faith. Of all people, a eucharistic minister's presence should communicate a deeply rooted joy.

The presence which the eucharistic minister carries, this divine presence, is a presence that communicates and nourishes faith. That is, this presence brings new life to the communicant's relationship with Christ. Those to whom we minister gain spiritual support and nourishment from the eucharist, of course, but they also gain support on the level of faith from the presence of the eucharistic minister.

The simple fact that you, the eucharistic minister, are there is a source of support for the faith of the person to whom you give Communion. Your commitment, your faithfulness, your willingness to be there when you are needed, your desire to share yourself and your time with others, all this nourishes and supports the faith of those whom you serve as a eucharistic minister.

In the late 1960s Peter L. Berger, a Lutheran sociologist, remarked in his book *The Sacred Canopy*, that in our society people who take their Christian faith to heart become, in sociological terms, "cognitive deviants." This simply means that our thinking deviates from the predominant, socially acceptable ways of thinking. In a society where things are a high priority, we give persons pride of place. In a society where violent solutions to conflict are common, we prefer to use force only as a last resort and with great reluctance. In a society where people are judged by their economic worth, we respect the dignity of all people regardless of socio-economic status. In a society where human beings have little value prior to birth and when they are old, we attribute equal value to human life from conception to natural death.

When we nourish the faith of those whom we serve as eucharistic ministers, this is not a pie-in-the-sky faith with little relevance to the realities of everyday existence. Rather, we nourish this faith which makes us, and them, "cognitive deviants" in our society. In some countries, where political forces mock religious freedom, eucharistic ministers could easily place their lives at great risk by simply doing what a eucharistic minister is supposed to do. In such societies, the presence of the eucharistic minister is a threat to political powers that fear the practical consequences of Christian faith.

The presence of the eucharistic minister is, in a special way, the presence of Christ. This is true not because of any special virtue or holiness on the part of the eucharistic minister; rather, it is because of your mission, your witness, and the gift of Holy Communion that you bring. There is room here only for humility. Yes, you share with others the eucharistic Christ, but you share only what you receive as a gift yourself. You bring the presence of Christ who gives himself to all equally.

As a eucharistic minister, your *mission* is to be the hands of Christ as he reaches out to nourish the faith of those who give themselves to him. When you allow yourself to be Christ's instrument you become a means by which Christ supports and encourages loving intimacy with him— which is the foundation of what we mean by "faith." To share Holy Communion with others is to allow the risen Christ to touch the hearts of his people in the most intimate way possible.

Your witness as a eucharistic minister is eucharistic, too. A "witness" is one who gives evidence or stands as a sign. In this case, as a eucharistic minister you stand as a sign of the eucharist itself, the gift of the risen Christ to his people, his gift of himself, "body and blood, soul and divinity." Because you are a sign of the eucharist, you are also a sign of all God's people, the church. So as a eucharistic minister you represent the local faith community, the parish, as well as the universal church.

This may seem an odd place to bring up the attire of the eucharistic minister, but your role as witness is affected by your appearance. It may seem obvious that when you act in your capacity as a eucharistic minister you should dress appropriately. Yet eucharistic ministers have been known to thoughtlessly distribute Communion dressed in an inappropriate manner.

A young male eucharistic minister wore very short cut-off jeans and tank top with a hole in it for a Saturday evening Mass in mid-July. Yes, it was a hot, humid evening, but his attire was out of line with what he was doing.

A middle-aged woman wore soiled slacks and a faded tee-shirt which advertised on the front her enthusiasm for a certain bowling alley. Not appropriate.

A well-meaning thirty-something male eucharistic minister presented himself at the bedside of an older hospitalized woman. He wore dirty work clothes, a greasy shirt, faded jeans with holes in them, and a sweat-stained baseball cap. Out of touch, fella.

How you dress when you act as a eucharistic minister declares to everyone your sense of dignity and decorum, as well as your respect for the eucharist itself. A tuxedo or formal gown—unless you are at a wedding Mass and are part of the wedding party—is just as inappropriate as clothes you would wear to clean out your basement. In most situations, wear neat, clean, modest attire that reflects reverence for the eucharist. Avoid both extreme formality and extreme informality. Obviously, be well groomed with clean hands and fingernails. For all this is a part of your witness as a eucharistic minister.

As a eucharistic minister, the *love* you share is basic to the special presence you bring. Your presence should not be characterized by sappy sentimentality or pious blather. G. K. Chesterton said a mouthful when he commented: "The way to love anything is to realise that it might be lost."

Your presence as a eucharistic minister may best be characterized by a love that takes its inspiration from Chesterton's remark. Your love will be real if it is conditioned by the realization that this person to whom you give Communion "might be lost." Think about it. When we take someone for granted is this not an act based on forgetting that this person "might be lost"? If we recall the person's mortality we gain more power to love him or her. We find it easier to be patient with even the most difficult person.

The presence of the risen Christ which you,

as a eucharistic minister, bring both in the sacrament and in yourself, is a presence characterized by a deeply spiritual, unromantic, realistic love. The best description of this love remains that given by St. Paul in 1 Corinthians:

> Love is patient; love is kind; love is not envious or boastful or arrogant or rude. It does not insist on its own way; it is not irritable or resentful; it does not rejoice in wrongdoing, but rejoices in the truth. It bears all things, believes all things, hopes all things, endures all things. Love never ends (13:4-7).

The presence we bring to our role as eucharistic ministers is rooted in this kind of love, a love that is no-nonsense and practical. It is a love which, to borrow the insight of St. Thomas Aquinas, seeks above all the good of the other. This is the love we bring to any situation in which we act as eucharistic ministers, whether during the eucharist or when we bring Communion to someone who is confined to home or to a hospital.

A few words from Psalm 105:4 make an ideal prayer for eucharistic ministers: "Seek the LORD and his strength; seek his presence continually."

This is what draws us to the eucharist, the desire to "seek the LORD and his strength," and the desire to "seek his presence continually."

As eucharistic ministers we serve the deep hunger people have to be nourished by the whole person of the risen Christ. We serve the deep thirst people have to be nourished by his presence. This is our ministry, and this is our privilege.

RESOURCES

A Body Broken for a Broken People: Eucharist in the New Testament, by Francis J. Moloney, S.D.B. Hendrickson Publishers, Revised edition, 1997.

The Church's Sacraments: Eucharist (pamphlet), by Joseph Martos. Liguori Publications, 1991.

The Dilemma of Priestless Sundays, by James Dallen. Liturgy Training Publications, 1994.

Doors to the Sacred: A Historical Introduction to Sacraments in the Catholic Church, Expanded Edition, by Joseph Martos. Triumph Books, 1991.

Eucharistic Minister (monthly newsletter), Beatrice Fleo, Editor. P.O. Box 419493, Kansas City, MO 64141-6493.

In the Presence of Our Lord: The History, Theology, and Psychology of Eucharistic Devotion, by Father Benedict J. Groeschel, C.F.R. and James Monti. Our Sunday Visitor Books, 1997.

Solemn Exposition of the Holy Eucharist. Liturgy Documentary Series 11. Publication No. 5-106. United States Catholic Conference, 1996.

Sunday Celebrations in the Absence of a Priest. Liturgy Documentary Series 10. Publication No. 5-105. United States Catholic Conference, 1996.

OTHER BOOKS BY MITCH FINLEY

Building Christian Families (with Kathy Finley;
 Thomas More Publications)

Catholic Spiritual Classics (Sheed & Ward)

*Your Family in Focus: Appreciating What You Have,
 Making It Even Better* (Ave Maria Press)

*Everybody Has a Guardian Angel...and Other Lasting Lessons
 I Learned in Catholic Schools* (Crossroad Publishing Co.)

Heavenly Helpers: St. Anthony and St. Jude
 (Crossroad Publishing Co.)

Catholic Is Wonderful (Resurrection Press)

Whispers of Love: Encounters with Deceased Relatives and Friends
 (Crossroad Publishing Co.)

Season of Promises (Resurrection Press)

Season of New Beginnings (Resurrection Press)

Surprising Mary (Resurrection Press)

The Joy of Being Catholic (Crossroad Publishing Co.)

The Seekers Guide to Being Catholic (Loyola Press)

PUBLISHED BY RESURRECTION PRESS

A Rachel Rosary *Larry Kupferman*	$3.95
Catholic Is Wonderful *Mitch Finley*	$4.95
Christian Marriage *John & Therese Boucher*	$3.95
Come, Celebrate Jesus! *Francis X. Gaeta*	$4.95
From Holy Hour to Happy Hour *Francis X. Gaeta*	$7.95
Healing through the Mass *Robert DeGrandis, SSJ*	$7.95
Healing the Wounds of Emotional Abuse *Nancy Benvenga*	$6.95
Healing Your Grief *Ruthann Williams, OP*	$7.95
Living Each Day by the Power of Faith *Barbara Ryan*	$8.95
Inwords *Mary Kraemer, OSF*	$4.50
The Healing of the Religious Life *Faricy/Blackborow*	$6.95
The Joy of Being a Catechist *Gloria Durka*	$4.50
Transformed by Love *Margaret Magdalen, CSMV*	$5.95
RVC Liturgical Series: The Liturgy of the Hours	$3.95
The Lector's Ministry	$3.95
Behold the Man *Judy Marley, SFO*	$4.50
Lights in the Darkness *Ave Clark, O.P.*	$8.95
Practicing the Prayer of Presence *van Kaam/Muto*	$7.95
5-Minute Miracles *Linda Schubert*	$3.95
Nothing but Love *Robert Lauder*	$3.95
Healthy and Holy under Stress *van Kaam/Muto*	$3.95
Season of New Beginnings *Mitch Finley*	$4.50
Season of Promises *Mitch Finley*	$4.50
Soup Pot *Ethel Pochocki*	$8.95
Stay with Us *John Mullin, SJ*	$3.95
Surprising Mary *Mitch Finley*	$7.95

For a free catalog call 1-800-892-6657